UNNAMED
AND
UNWANTED...
(What Am I Here For?)

CHERISE STEVENSON

Possibilities Publishing is a subsidiary of Ark of Safetea.

Email: possibiliteapublishing@gmail.com

Cover/Back cover design: Viviana Salgado of Studio Creative Group

www.studiocreativegroup.com email: Viviana a studio creative group.com

Write the author Cherise Stevenson

Email: nyevangelist@yahoo.com

For more information about special discounts, for bulk purchases, please contact nyevangelist@yahoo.com

ISBN:1547034750
ISBN-13:978-1547034758

DEDICATION

This book is dedicated to the "Silent Sufferers."
I (you) shall not die but live, and declare the works of the Lord.
(Psalm 118:17).

AUTOGRAPH PAGE

ACKNOWLEDGMENTS

My biological Father: First and foremost, I want to say thank you for being you and true to yourself. Because of your absence, drug abuse and denial that I even exist, I don't even know your name. Even though I was robbed of having a grandfather, God saw fit to allow Isaiah Stevenson to be my "daddy." This is the man I compare all the men in my life to and I thank God for that.

My biological Mother Jeanine Ernestine: I thank you for your determination and being true to your word. Ironically, I guess I get that from you. You were determined not to have me, and you did just that. An abortion didn't work, so you allowed someone else to raise me. Doris wasn't the best, but she stepped up and accepted the responsibility to raise a child that wasn't biologically hers. And for that, she earned the privilege to be called and honored as "mommy."

I forgive you both.

A REAL MOTHER'S LOVE

There are not enough words to say or enough love to display my gratefulness to those of you who thought it not robbery to give me what I needed when I needed it the most.

Thank You...

Jackie Brooks (deceased), Lucille Burgess, LaVerne Gamble, Edna Morgan, Elder Marsha Byers, Diane Utendahl (deceased), Janet James (deceased), Elder Mary Smith (deceased), Anne Graham (deceased), Elder Barbara Mayo, Evg. Susie Gray Goldson (deceased), Lady Tracy Hopkins, Freida Wilson, Evg. Rosalyn Fields (deceased), Justina White, Elder Judy Lesley, Ethelmae Culver, Zelda Williams, Tonja (Wiggles) Ottley, Renee Moore, Lady Monique Williams-Walker, Pastor Subrenia McDaniel, Pastor Yvonne Jones.

FOREWORD

I am beyond privileged to write this foreword on behalf of one of the most giving, committed and loyal people I know. I have been gifted with the ministry that is Cherise in the early 2000s, and since receiving that gift – I have been overwhelmed with joy, laughter, love, favor and Godly counsel. I'm sure that any of you privileged to know her can say the same thing. You know folks are true blue when they help you plan and execute a homegoing service for a cat – down to the last detail – even getting "Funeral" stickers for the motorcade... for a cat .... yup, you read that right ... for a cat!

While the title of the book is her experience of being "unnamed" and "unwanted", her life now is a testimony that God indeed had other plans for her (Jeremiah 29:11). I know beyond knowing that this book is a requisite part of the Ministry that God has placed in her and Reader, know this one thing: God is no Respecter of persons. What He will do in the life of one, He will certainly do in yours. Cherise's life now is one of tremendous favor, courage and wisdom. She knows her name and others do too. She is highly sought after because when Cherise is around, you can be sure that things will run decently and in order and she continues to grow because God is certainly not through with her and He's not through with you either!

If you need encouragement that God can do mighty things in the life of one whom man has discounted – read this book; if you need assurance that God will never leave you or forsake you – read this book; if you need proof that God will elevate you beyond even your wildest dreams – read this book; if you need an example that God will make your name known among the most important of people – read this book! Then after you've read it, believe God and stay tuned. The Word says that we should follow those who through faith and patience have inherited the promises

(Hebrews 6:12). I encourage you to follow Cherise's Ministry, because He is about to do some amazing things for and through her. Be encouraged Reader and stay steadfast in your faith!

Cherise, as you continue to go forward in Ministry, continually meditate on the fact that God knew you before anyone else, and it is His Perfect Will that you play a role in ensuring that our women of tomorrow grow into His Perfect Will as well. Don't doubt your calling. Don't doubt your name and whatever you do, don't ever doubt that you are wanted! I give God the praise for you continually and am so Godly proud of the way that you let God use you through this book.

To GOD be the Glory for the Things that He has done!

Rev. Dr. Leisa Herrera

Senior Pastor

Kingdom City Fellowship

UNNAMED & UNWANTED

FOUNDATION OF DYSFUNCTION: FAMILY TREE

ISAIAH STEVENSON (MARRIED) LUCILLE GILLMORE

Isaiah Jr.   David   Richard   Lawrence   Joan   Jeanine
(Deceased) *(Deceased)*   *(Deceased)*

~DIVORCED~

ISAIAH STEVENSON (JOINED) DORIS BLAKE-WISE (STEVENSON)

Lorraine   Douglas   Francis (Butch)   +   Jeanine (Isaiah's daughter)
(Deceased) *(Deceased)*   *(Deceased)*

Side Note: When Isaiah joined, (not married) Doris, he took Jeanine, his youngest daughter with him. Even though Jeanine had biological brothers and a sister, she was raised very closely with Doris' three children. Because of this bond and Jeanine being my biological mother, Doris' children became my uncles and aunt: her grandchildren became my cousins and so forth. I had no idea the first set of aunt and uncles even existed. I believe because Isaiah and Doris were previously married, it was a mutual decision to just "be" together. This "togetherness" lasted for 37 years, literally until death did they part. Now on with my testimony.....

DECADE ONE – 1970'S: "UNWANTED YET KEPT"

Jeremiah 1:5 "...before I formed you in the womb I knew you; before you were born I sanctified you..."

June 16, 1970, as far as I am concerned, is the greatest day in history (excluding the birth, burial, and resurrection of Jesus Christ). This day is so extraordinary that I decided to tell you about it. You see, this is the day that I, Cherise Stevenson, was born. What's so special about that? It's special because when momma said no, God said yes! As it was told to me, Jeanine, my biological mother, didn't want to have me. Jeanine had my oldest brother, Edward, and gave him to his grandmother on his father's side to raise him. I have no idea how he ended up with Isaiah and Doris. Jeanine became pregnant three more times, but she aborted them. You would think after the first child, that she would have used some form of contraceptive. But when you're strung out on drugs, common sense goes out the window. When Jeanine became pregnant for the fifth time, 5 being the number of grace, she made her usual appointment to have an abortion. Because she had already had three procedures back to back, the doctor denied her request. Jeanine was so busy getting high and drunk that she wasn't properly taking care of her body. Therefore, to save herself, she had to carry and give birth to this child. I am 210% sure she was beyond upset. This pregnancy meant that Jeanine would have to give up the things she loved the most: smoking, drinking, and sex. Honestly, I really don't think she cared.

Now the time has come for the delivery to take place. I'm not too sure about this theory, but I am almost positive because of what I was told. I was born in the house. The address that the hospital put on my birth certificate is incorrect. The theory is this: Jeanine was so incoherent that she didn't realize that she had gone into labor or that her water broke. By the time someone noticed what was going on, it was too late. I do believe that someone called the paramedics. They took Jeanine and the baby to the hospital. Jeanine had given birth to a baby girl. That's all she knew. Jeanine didn't know how to check in, but she sure knew how to check out. I don't think she even got herself examined. She just left. Yes, she left me in the hospital. What? Oh, you thought that because she gave birth, she would have a change of heart. Please note that in order for change to take place one must first have a heart. Remember, she didn't want the baby in the first place. Jeanine didn't know that because of her drug use, I was born with abdominal complications and almost died. She didn't even give me a name. I was in the hospital for a few days. I was sick, nameless and homeless. I don't know who said what or who did what, but finally I had a home and parents. And thanks to one of my cousins, I also had a name: Cherise.

Now, thanks to the "family tree" you know that Isaiah and Doris are my grandparents. But as a child I didn't know that. I don't know how exactly the transition of parents happened, but Isaiah and Doris were my daddy and mother. And I have a big brother named Edward who was five years older than me. For a long time, I thought that they birthed him as well. As far as I can remember, growing up was great. We lived in a house in the

Bronx across from Crotona Park. I had two dogs, Duke and Tuffy, and a cat named Tiger. I remember my brother lost Tuffy in the park because he wanted to play basketball. I remember Duke always ate Sunday's dinner while we were at church. I remember Tiger being a bully, and would make Duke catch the mice in the house. Seriously. You read that right: my cat Tiger would make my German Shepherd, Duke, chase and catch the mice, and then bring it to him so he could play with it.

I also remember the difference in attentiveness between me and my brother, that was given by our mother. I remember getting beat with a hair brush every night. I was made to say my prayers, but not him. I remember my brother getting in trouble a lot, but still able to do, go and have whatever he wanted. I remember him going to Boy Scouts. I remember him being able to bring home the class pet for weekends. It didn't matter though because my brother was my best friend. He would always play with me, and make me laugh especially after I got a beating. His favorite thing to do with me was tickle me. Once he did that, everything was better. But there was one incident that took place back then that is very evident to this day that I was "unwanted" or irrelevant to say the least. This particular year, my brother's birthday and Easter were on the same day. He was turning eleven. My mother threw him the biggest birthday party EVER! Family and friends came over. My mother cooked everything she could possibly think of: collard greens, mac & cheese, string beans, black eyed peas, yams, a turkey, several hams, macaroni salad, potato salad, several different flavored cakes, sweet potato pies and banana pudding because that was his favorite. Each and every dish was made from scratch. She pulled out the good crystal punch bowl set to make some red Kool-Aid with soda in it. All of this for an eleven-year-old boy, who was acting up in school and always in trouble. Needless to say, when my birthday came, all I received was a chocolate cake, which was my favorite. No party. No special dinner. No gathering of family and friends. No gifts. Just cake. Oh yeah, and a beating with a hair brush to say my prayers.

Not many months later, we moved from the house to the projects.   The only thing that changed was my address.   My brother was still mischievous, and I was still ostracized. I will admit that I started hoping he would get in trouble really bad, and get a beating like I did instead of just getting yelled at.

One day after school, my mother took me to a hospital. She explained to me that my daddy was sick, and we were going to see him. I found out later that my daddy had a heart attack. Never in a thousand years would I have imagined that this would begin the worst times of my life. Not because my daddy was in the hospital, but because of the people his hospital stays brought to surface. By this time, I was about eight and my brother was a teenager with his own agenda. Even though I was young I was rather intelligent. Even with all of my intellect, one rule always remained the same: whatever my mother said, that's what it was.

So, when I heard my mother on the phone with someone demanding that they needed to go see their father in the hospital because he was asking for her, I paid it no mind. I don't remember if it was the next day or a few days after that phone call, but some woman showed up claiming to have gone seen "daddy", and was introduced to me as a friend of the family named Jeanine.

When I asked my brother about her, he avoided the question with an "I don't know", and that was the end of it. I remember when Jeanine showed up at the house. Everyone was very relaxed and comfortable around this "stranger" except me. Apparently, everyone "knew" of this family friend, but me. This "one-time visit" turned into an on-again, off-again residency for the next couple of years in our two-bedroom apartment in the projects, with her three children who were younger than me. It was already bad enough that my mischievous brother was my mother's golden child, now I had to share my space with strangers. I had to speak and be friendly with people I didn't know. I had to share room space, sleeping space, eating space, and bathroom time. I had to constantly repeat, "don't touch my stuff", and I became an automatic babysitter. I had to take them everywhere I went. UGH!!! At this age, I didn't understand what frustration or aggravation was, but I know that I was probably demonstrating it with my behavior and yelling all the time. "Now I lay me down to sleep. I pray the Lord my soul to keep. If I should die before I wake, I pray the Lord my soul to take." I got it. I no longer need to be beaten with the hair brush.

DECADE TWO – 1980'S: "SOVEREIGN GOD"

Psalm 46:1 "God is our refuge and strength, a very present help in the time of trouble."

Are you familiar with the "80/20 rule?" It states that 80% of outcomes can be attributed to 20% of the causes for a given event. You mostly hear of this rule concerning marriages, relationships or businesses. Whelp, I'd like to apply it to another aspect of life: parenting.

My mother was definitely a good mother to anyone who watched and viewed from the outside. I was clean, well dressed, well behaved, well spoken, and well mannered. I ate three meals a day, slept in a bed, went to the top schools in the Bronx, never missed a doctor's appointment, was taught how to clean and maintain a home. This is great and there is nothing missing, right? Wrong. That was it. That was the extent of her version of motherhood towards me. This was her 20% of parenting. So then, what's the 80% that's missing? I'm glad you asked. There was no nurturing, no bonding, no support, no encouragement, no comfort, no understanding, no communication, no hugs, no kisses, and definitely no "I love you" EVER. The only time we held meaningful conversations was when she was being nosy. And if it was real juicy, I was rewarded, usually with staying up past my curfew.

On the other hand, there was my daddy. The opposite, the balance, but not completely 100% either. His 20% was the fact that I felt that he didn't speak up enough on my behalf when my mother would tell him some nonsense about me misbehaving or being disrespectful towards her. Ironically, he said nothing. He would simply ignore her and go out with the guys while I remained in the house being cleverly tortured with my mother's mean and harsh words. But his 80% was phenomenal! Between my brother and my daddy, everyone knew who I was, and they had better not mess with me! My daddy was my greatest love, and my biggest fan! He supported everything I did, whether he agreed or not. One of the most important things my daddy did for me was at the age of 10, he taught me how to read and understand the King James Version of the Bible. My daddy taught me that the red lettering in the Bible was when Jesus was speaking. He also taught me what is known as The Lord's Prayer. And for his own pleasurable reasons, my daddy showed me all the "cuss" words in the Bible such as damn, hell, ass. I remember him laughing real hard every time he read them because I would say, "Oooooo, you said a bad word!" He would say, "No it's not because it's in the Bible." So, they were good words when it's in the Bible, but when I said them they were bad words? To a ten-year-old, they were the same damn words! I was confused, but that was our on-going joke. Hilarious. The timing of me learning to comprehend the Bible could not have been more profound and precise. It was also at age 10 that I heard my mother saying she didn't want me, and she wished I wasn't there. It was also the first time I heard her call me a bitch. She was in the kitchen talking and drinking with a friend. I heard it as I was approaching the kitchen for something, probably for something to eat or drink. As I was leaving the kitchen, I heard her say "She ain't gonna be nothing just like her mother." Really?! That's how you feel about a 10-year-old? What did I do to deserve such nastiness? I couldn't wait for my daddy to get home. It was too late to go anywhere. I just stayed in my room with my dolls, TV, and my thoughts of how to punch her in the face and get away it. If she was my mother, why would she call herself nothing? I don't know how to describe the pain I felt. I wished I had a grandmother to go to, and she could raise me like some of my friends had. I decided that I must have done something to make my mother say those things. So, I was determined to be the best child ever. If I did that, she would love and want me. I had a plan. I didn't need my daddy. Everything was going to be alright.

Years passed, time went on, and everything wasn't and hadn't been alright. Jeanine and her brood moved in. My space and peace of mind were invaded. My brother was more reckless. My daddy stayed out more, and derogatory actions and comments were still made to and about me. I guess my mother felt since Jeanine moved in, she had an audience 24 hours/7 days a week. And with Jeanine in need of a residence for herself and her brood, she obliged. This went on every day while they indulged in Budweiser with Georgi Vodka chasers, and smoking Salem cigarettes. Not once can I recall Jeanine telling or asking my mother to not say such nasty things or to stop calling me a bitch. In the beginning, you saw the family tree, but keep in mind that I was still a child and had no idea of the truth.......yet.

One weekend my mother sponsored a bus trip to Atlantic City.

She was a member of the Eastern Stars, and my daddy was a Mason. Being 14 now, as long as I did what my mother said, she left me alone, but her mouth was still unmentionable. She always had to say something to prove who was in charge. She was the boss. As my mother laid down the house rules, Jeanine was simply to oversee the house, keep her brood in check, and my mother told me once I finished my chores, I could go outside with my friends. Again, MY MOTHER SAID I COULD GO OUTSIDE. No problem. My parents left. I began to do my chores. I don't recall what everyone else was doing, and honestly I wasn't concerned. Because I knew this trip was coming, I already made plans with my crew, and had the timing of everything I needed to do down to a science. To give me energy I played my favorite music which was a bunch of music recorded from off the radio onto a cassette tape like: Jungle Brothers "I'll House Ya", Scott La Rock "Criminal Minded" and Rob Base "Joy and Pain". I was feeling good, real good because I had been planning this for months. I was in such a flow that I actually finished ahead of schedule. So now my chores were completed, and my home was immaculate. I showered and was getting dressed. My entire outfit matched to perfection, even down to my undergarments. I was dancing and prancing around in my room while putting the finishing touches on myself. I was about to head out to meet my crew, and Jeanine took it upon herself to enter my room. Actually, I think she had been standing there for quite some time watching me. I normally didn't speak to her when my mother was there, so I definitely wasn't holding a conversation with her now. Especially when I had plans and was ahead of schedule. I remember her standing there trying to have a conversation with me. That bothered me a little because when my mother was here, she doesn't say anything to me except, "What you want from the store?" My mother sends me to go get her beer and cigarettes. So why was she talking to me now? I remember mumbling "thank you" because it sounded like she gave me a compliment. It was like I heard her, but I wasn't listening. I didn't want to say too much because then she would think that we could talk and that wasn't gonna happen, especially today.

One thing is for sure was that she was getting on my nerves standing in my bedroom doorway. After I gave myself a final look-over, I proceeded to leave. Strangely enough, Jeanine did not move from the doorway. Because my mother raised me to have manners, I said, "Excuse me." She asked me where I thought I was going, and did not move out of the way. I was trying to figure out what went wrong. I thought she gave me a compliment; I said thank you. She was in my way. I said excuse me, and she didn't move. I stood there really confused, and I am sure my facial expression showed it because I know she heard my mother say that after I finished my chores, I could go outside. This delay was interfering with my schedule. I was out of manners and patience. I had no control over my attitude. So, with disgust, I repeated what my mother said while still trying to pass by her standing in the doorway. What happened next, I don't quite remember, but I believe she said something to the fact that I wasn't going anywhere. I probably snatched her up without thinking about it. I didn't even know my brother was back in the house. He either heard the commotion or her children said something, but by the time my brother reached my room, Jeanine was already on the floor, and I had her in a position to snap her neck. My brother taught me that move from watching wrestling and Bruce Lee. NEVER in a million years did I think would hear what I heard next. "Cherise! GET OFF YOUR MOTHER LIKE THAT!" While still holding Jeanine in position, and not loosening the grip, I looked at my brother and the clock, because by this time, he should have had his morning and afternoon balance of weed. And if you know anything about weed heads is that the more they smoke, the more intellectual they become. Sometimes they make really good sense! So, I asked him what he said. Again, he said, "Let go of your mother." I said, "What are you talking about? Mommy is in Atlantic City. You helped her carry her stuff and loaded the bus." He said, "Yea, that's mommy, but that's not your real mother. Jeanine is your real mother. Cherise, let her go, she can't breathe." I never knew my brother to lie to me before, so why would he lie to me now? I finally let her go and watched her struggle to get up while holding her neck and gasping for air. My attitude was unexplainable at this point. I had to redo me all over again, and my friends were waiting for me.

While getting dressed again, I asked my brother why did he say that. "Because it's true," he said. I asked, "Why didn't you say something before I was about to break her neck?" He said, "It wasn't important until now, and I thought mom or dad was gonna tell you." I said, "I'm gonna ask them when they get back. Wait! Them kids are my brothers and sister???" "Yeah," he said. That was the end of the conversation. My brother helped her up and made sure she left the room with him. I guess my questions were interfering with his high. Everything went back to normal like nothing happened. My brother said that like it wasn't supposed to affect me. And, why should it? It didn't bother him. He already knew the truth. What was I supposed to do with this information? How was I supposed to feel? What do I say to Jeanine? Or to the kids? Thoughts and emotions were beyond out of control. Maybe I should've stayed and talked to her. As I finished my hair, I decided on an emotion to dwell in....HATE. I left out the house without saying anything to anyone. I know "hate" is a strong word, but in my defense, I had six years to think back on, build and create it. Remember I first met Jeanine at age 8, when my daddy had his first heart attack. Then Jeanine hustled and hung around for the next 6 years in our home knowing who I was to her and never said a word. Now the comments and the kitchen conversations that always seemed to end whenever I came around made sense. Now the mystery of why her children looked like me and my brother, even though we're not "related" was solved. Now I understand why Jeanine could come and go as she pleased. It's one thing to be abandoned at birth and not know your parents. It's something totally different to be in the presence of your biological parent for 6 years, and not know it. Or to join in with the individuals who spoke against and emotionally tore

15

down your child because you needed a place to stay and your habit supported. I saw many TV shows, but never thought I would ever have to ask why she didn't want me? Why she didn't love me? What was wrong with me? Why did everyone else know the truth about me, but ME?"

I still went out, but really couldn't enjoy myself. My perfect day was ruined. Well, except for the drinking, the boys and the outfit. The earlier part of the day just kept playing over and over in my mind. When I returned home, Jeanine and her brood were so still and quiet, you would have thought I lived alone. I just went straight to my room. Finally, I heard my parents come in. I immediately got out of my bed and went to the kitchen. I couldn't wait another second to get to the bottom of this story, and bring this horrible day to an end. My daddy went straight to bed because we had church in the morning. So, I went straight to my mother. I was still upset, so I got right to the point and asked if Jeanine was my real mother. My mother asked who told me that, and I told her my brother said it when me and Jeanine had a fight. Now she wanted to know what happened. After I explained the day, all she could say was, "Yes, it's true." She quickly dismissed the conversation and sent me to bed. Just like that. So, you being my mother is not prompting you to ask if I was okay or how was I feeling? You really don't care about me at all? How come no one wanted to talk and tell me the truth? Why was everyone okay with this outcome? Why was this a secret? What did they think would happen once I found out? What was I supposed to do with this information? How was I supposed to act around the kids and this woman? I went back to bed and I remember that I didn't sleep well. While on our way to church, I asked my daddy. Finally, the truth. My daddy gave me words of comfort and understanding to the best of his ability, but looking back I can clearly see that it was God that shielded and covered me from the sting of death, that a situation like that could have caused. I guess my parents just wanted to leave well enough alone and that's just what they did. It was moments like this where I wish I had grandparents to go and stay with. It was never mentioned again after that night.

I didn't want to be home with them. I became the busiest person in the church besides the pastor. I was teaching Sunday School, secretary of the Sunday School Department, and president of the youth department which included the Junior usher boards, choirs, and young people equaling almost 100 people in total. And yes, I was still 14. I also remember me and my crew got saved, received the right hand of fellowship, and was baptized. The good ole` days. I was flourishing in church, and things couldn't be more wrong at home. So much so, that church became my escape, my refuge, and my freedom. I thought I didn't know how to pray, not realizing that every time I called on the name of Jesus that was prayer!

After the news bomb of "who's who", Jeanine and her brood left. My mother also put my brother out. So now that just left me in the house. My cousin, the one who named me, and her two boys finally got their own place, so they left as well. Yes, for a season, there were three families living under one roof in a two-bedroom apartment in the projects. Now it was just me. My mother was so violently verbal that when she wasn't belittling me or cursing, I thought something was wrong, and I was right. That's how I knew she was sick or in the process of having an asthma attack. If for nothing else, I knew my mother was highly upset that her one-woman show was over because her audience of one, Jeanine, was gone. Other than that, everything was my fault. For example, I would be in school and get yelled at when I got home because something happened during the day that upset her. I even got cussed out for stuff my brother did! I remember one day he was mad at my mother because she wouldn't give him any money to go get some sneakers. So, he went in her purse, took her keys and locked her inside the house! He hid her keys in the mailbox. I got in trouble and cussed out for laughing. By the way, that still makes me giggle. The ultimate state of crazy/dysfunction/bipolar from my mother was, "DON'T YOU HEAR ME TALKING TO YOU? THEN ANSWER ME! WHAT DID YOU SAY? ANSWER ME! DID YOU JUST SASS ME? THINK YOU KNOW EVERYTHING. DON'T TALK WHILE I'M TALKING! NOW YOU HAVE NOTHING TO SAY? YOU SO SMART, YOU STUPID." And all of this was said without me saying not one word. She would have these conversations all by herself, every day.

One Sunday on our way home from church, I asked my daddy

a bunch of questions. I just exploded because I felt like I was going crazy and he was always calm, cool and collected. Didn't we all live in the same house? How could you NOT hear this, and not be affected or angry? But then I remembered that she only "performed" when he wasn't in the house so he really didn't get to see her in rare form. He got the "Oh, Cherise did this and Cherise did that" stories. Besides drinking until he became deaf to her voice, my daddy said this one thing that, to me at that time, made more sense than the Bible! He simply said "It takes two to argue. Either way, your mother is going to be right, so why bother?" Yes, she spoke to my daddy in the same manner. My daddy also explained that this was the reason he stayed out with the fellas. Got it! Don't argue, get drunk and stay out until she went to sleep. Well, I managed 2 out of 3. Unlike these kids today, I had a curfew and nightly chores at age 14, so I had to kick the "stay out" part of the plan to the curb. But trust and believe I mastered the other two.

OH MY GOODNESS!!!! The day every teenage girl waits for, her 16th BIRTHDAY! My daddy took care of his obligations which were my "age" corsage and money. My friends from school LITERALLY threw me a party on the back of the Bronx 36 bus, down to a JVC boom box. Remember those? I guess you can say it was a breakfast party because there was baconeggcheese, yes, one word, on a roll, and bagels with cream cheese and jelly with Tropicana orange juice everywhere! Instead of cake someone brought donuts from Dunkin Donuts. I had the best day at school!

Because it was my birthday I was excused from gym. After my attendance was taken in homeroom, thanks to all the security guards and Officer Williams, I could hangout all day. All the guys who thought they were my boyfriend either fed me or gave me money. The highlight of that portion of the day was that the guys at school thought they were going to be the one to give me my "special" gift. I took too much pleasure in telling them all NO. I lost some male friends behind that, but oh well. I was a church girl and I was scared of God! I remember having so much fun! My friends really made my 16th birthday memorable. And so did my mother. I came home to absolutely nothing. I can accept not having a party at age 11 like my brother because after all, his birthday fell on Easter. But this was my 16th birthday. A sweet 16 supposedly.

My outfit was questioned, a multi-colored shirt dress and some heels, but not complimented. I think she mumbled happy birthday. Okay, so no party. But she didn't even invite my crew to the house for dinner. I guess the fact that she did cook some of my favorite dishes should have been enough. Oh, and I was possibly one less of a bitch than on any other day. And my annual chocolate cake. Here I am 16, doing very well in school, in church, had a job, catered to her every need and want, and she couldn't even appreciate or celebrate me on my special day? I was never more embarrassed and humiliated. What was I going to tell my friends when they asked, "what did your mother get you for your birthday?" Good thing about my friends were they actually already knew the outcome which is why they did all they could to make my happy. I do believe subconsciously something within me snapped. I still wasn't bluntly disrespectful, just mumbled a little louder, but I did become vindictive, laced with irony of words. Being that my mother had bronchial asthma due to a collapsed lung, her sensitivity of certain smells would trigger an attack almost immediately. Once I figured that out, by accident, I used it to my advantage. My favorite "smell" was nail polish or the nail polish remover. Whenever I had enough of the "bitch-calling" for the day, and dinner was done, I would open it up. I did NOT USE it. I would just let the aroma float from my bedroom to the kitchen where my mother was. It would be all of ten minutes before the cussing and gasping for breath would start. "STOP POLISHING YOUR *&^%$&%& NAILS IN THIS HOUSE!" I would then go to the kitchen and show her that my nails were dry and I wasn't using any polish. By then, she could care less. All she needed at that moment was an ambulance. I would call, they would come and just like that I was at peace for at least 5 to 7 days. After that first high of peace, I realized that I wanted it again. So then I began to not polish my nails at least once a month.

I'll admit it: I became a peace junkie, and rehab was not needed. Because I couldn't keep sending my mother to the hospital every other week, I found other ways to become creative. Since she already believed the worst about me, I began to create situations at school that caused me to stay late for in-house detentions, or something always happened on my commute home: fights, bus broke down, sick passenger – whatever. I would also purposely miss curfew and stay at someone's house. I didn't do that one too often because then my punishment would be that I couldn't go to church. Eventually I found an honest way to spend the night out and still go to church. I spent the night at my cousin Vonné's house. At this point and age, my resources of peace were very crucial. My mother's verbalization was at its pinnacle of challenge, and I honestly didn't know how much more I could take. Not only did the name calling and belittling continue, but now came the phrase, "I can't wait for her to get out of my house." No matter how horrific the delivery of the statement was, it was the first time ever that I actually AGREED! YES, YES, OH GOD YES, I must get out of her house! All of a sudden the nastiness and negativity no longer mattered because in a few months, I wouldn't have to deal with it any more. She became my motivation to do whatever needed to be done to go to college. I was beside myself with excitement, that every time I heard her tell someone that she couldn't wait for me to get out of her %$&^ &^ %$ house, I would chime in, "me neither!" I met with guidance counselors to make sure my credits were accounted for and up to date. I filled out every college application that was connected with business administration.

As I followed up with my progress, I found out that I accumulated more than enough credits to graduate early, I passed all my regents and I was being honored during my graduation ceremony! Everything was coming together better than I expected! I was too hyped! I was finally leaving the house of damnation! One day, I was talking with my friends and they were talking about the colleges they were accepted to. Wait a minute? Where were my acceptance letters? Surely, if anyone should be receiving acceptance letters, it should have been ME! It didn't make sense to ask my daddy because all he did was go to work and give my mother money to take care of the house. I had to speak to my mother. It took me a few days to approach her about it because I didn't know what to expect, and I had to honor her like the Bible said. "Ma, did you get any mail for me from any of the schools I applied to?" She said, "No, you ain't get no damn mail and you not going to get any mail from them either." "Why not?" I asked her. She said, "Because I didn't sign the forms to complete your financial aid." I think this was actually the first real big argument I had with her. I mumbled from time to time, but this here was face to face confrontation. I HAD IT! She had crushed my one and only way of escape and going forward in my career of becoming an Administrator. I felt my life was over and there was no escape from this madness. We argued and I left and stayed out until my daddy came home. Needless to say, from that day forward, the tension in the house was inevitable. The only conversation in the house was when my mother wanted something from the store. My daddy stayed out more, and so did I. All that was left to do was to be cordial because I remembered that my mother put my brother out, and I wasn't ready for that.

FINALLY! FINALLY! FINALLY! HIP HOP HOORAY! IT'S MY GRADUATION DAY!!! I was very proud of myself, but I was prouder of my twin, my bestie, my cousin, Vonné. She had become pregnant at 16, but didn't drop out of school. Our graduation was on the same day just at different times. I was in the morning, and she was at night. Even though I woke up sick with an ear infection. Who does that? I was put on bed rest, but I was still excited about graduation. I was among the top 83% graduating class, and was being honored with awards for regents and perfect attendance. I had the privilege to sit on stage with keynote guests and the principal. There was no way I was missing this! The only thing worse than being bed-ridden sick on your graduation day was my mother. She believed I was sick and actually wanted me to stay home, but couldn't accept the fact that I was being honored at my high school graduation. Apparently, I was a liar and forged documents (with the school seal on them) that were mailed to the house in a sealed envelope. She had the audacity to tell me to my face, "This must be a joke. Why would they want to honor you? I gotta see this for myself because you ain't all that smart." I was numb due to my medication, so I heard her, but I didn't hear her. I made a mental note to address that later. I was moving slow because those were the best meds ever, I managed to make it through graduation. As bad as I felt, it was the best day ever! As being president over the youth dept. at church, I was always appreciated, but this was the first time I actually appreciated myself. I graduated with honors. Finished school in January, walked with my June graduates. Surely celebration was in order! And it was. It just didn't come from my mother. She had an attitude because she was proven wrong about my accomplishments. No party. No dinner. Not even the infamous chocolate cake. I went to see my aunt D to kill time, and get my monetary gift. After that I went to my twin Vonné's graduation. The two underdogs came out on top! It was with her and my friends that I celebrated for the next three days. I partied my sickness away.

Eventually, reality set in, and I knew I had to find something to do or somewhere to go. Otherwise, one of us was going to check-out of here before their time, and it wasn't going to be me. I ended up attending Lehman College. Shockingly, my mother signed the paperwork for completion. Til this day, I will never understand why she didn't sign the other applications. Once classes started, I felt there still wasn't enough distance between her and I, so I went and got a job. That felt perfect. I was gone before she got up, and didn't return until she was asleep. I hung out on the weekends and yes, still made it to church. Somehow, someway, in the midst of me schooling and working, Jeanine slipped back in the house, but this time without her brood. Through bits and pieces of conversation, I found out that her children were back in foster care and when she went to go get them, they told her they didn't want to be with her. So now my house is back to having two drunken, cussing women. I need to either take more classes or do overtime. Conversations were more explicated than any French or Italian could ever imagine.

One Saturday, after I had done all I needed to do, I was on my way out for the weekend. My mother was talking to me, stopping me from leaving. As she was speaking, she kept calling me a bitch. When I'd had enough, I politely asked her to stop calling me that. Then the conversation became irate, and she was up in my face trying to provoke me to hit her. I thought to myself "okay, she added a new act to her show. I guess she was trying to impress Jeanine." When she wouldn't stop, I said to her, "Today is the last day you will call me a bitch. I'm leaving." She replied, "Well if you're leaving then only take what you brought. As a matter of fact, give me that jacket. I brought that." So now, I have not only a decision, but a final decision to make. Was my mother joking or was she really going to make me take this jacket off? Better yet, was I really going to do it? Was I going to stand my ground? After standing there with my mother face to face for like what seemed to have been an eternity, I took the jacket off and let it fall to the floor, went and put on my long, black leather trench that I brought with my money and left.

DECADE THREE – 1990'S: "UNMERITED FAVOR"

Psalm 91:14 "Because he has set his love upon me, therefore I will deliver him...."

Wow. Did that just happen? Did I just walk out of my mother's house? Here I was 19, a few months before my twentieth birthday and I had officially just left my mother's house. Cherise, did you really take off that jacket and drop it on the floor? Yeah girl, you're fed up. You had it. Now what? First go find my daddy and tell him what happened. I remember my college friend, Lei told me I could stay with her if I needed to. I sure hope she meant that because she was the first person I reached out to. After speaking with my daddy, who was not happy about me leaving, but was relieved at the same time, I went to Lei's house to speak with her and her parents. On my way to her house, I found myself talking to God and remembering His word: "Okay God, I am still in shock of what just happened, and I don't know what is going to happen, but I need you. You said, "honor thy mother and father that my days may be long in the land," Exodus 20:12. God you know I did that and it was hard! I hate to leave my daddy, but she was gonna make me hurt her. You said, "When your mother and father forsake you, You would take me up," Psalm 27:10. Well God, I've been forsaken by my mother and I need your help. Please let everything be alright with me staying at Lei's house. Amen." I finally arrived at Lei's house and as I've done before, I stayed the weekend. Told Lei what happened, which explained why I had no clothes with me. We wore the same size so that was solved easily. After listening, and both of us crying, Lei decided for us to get a place together. I wasn't working at the time, so we had to present a solid case to her parents in order for this to work, and for them to say yes. We presented our case to her parents, explained what happened to me, that I was still in school, and was applying for public assistance. After much questioning and drilling, Lei's parents saw that we were very sure, confident and thought things through. They finally said yes, and gave us their blessings and support. THANK YOU, JESUS! I was able to stay there until we found a place, which took about a month. That was one of the best months I have had in a long time. There was nothing that me and Lei didn't do. We sat up all night talking like we didn't have school in the morning, wearing her clothes, hanging out on the weekends. I was almost embarrassed to have this much fun. But then there were times where it would actually sadden me because I couldn't understand why I couldn't or didn't have this type of love and support from my own mother, but a stranger loved me so easily and freely. Why was it so hard for my mother to love me? I had not gone to see my mother or spoken with her once I left. All I could do was hope and pray that my daddy and my niece were alright. After me and Lei signed our lease, and I had keys of my own, I decided that it was time to go to my mother's house. That one month went by so fast! I guess it is true that time flies when you're having fun! It didn't make sense to me to carry all my things and clutter up Lei's house only to move it out again. All kinds of back-flips were going on in my tummy, as I dreaded knocking on my mother's door. As she opened the door she said "I knew you'd be back. Don't nobody want you." Strangely enough, you would think she wouldn't let me in, but she opened the door wide enough for me to pass right on by her, as almost to say, "I missed you." Jeanine was still there. Both of them were just sitting at the table in the kitchen, smoking and drinking. I said hello as I entered and went straight to my old room. The pain I felt that I had to leave my home in such a disarray of emotions was eating at me like cancer. My daddy wasn't there. My niece was so happy to see me. I remember speaking with her and trying to explain to a 2-year-old that I no longer lived there. That was one of the hardest things I had to do. That little girl was trying to talk my ear off and get me to play with everything! I gathered everything I could take with me this one time because after this I would not be back.

My mother followed me into the room questioning and mocking me, and making sure I only took what I brought with my money. If I picked up something, she would immediately say "put that back, I brought that" as to really hurt me or prove a point. My mother was really hoping that I would fail and would need to come back to her house. But because I was packing, she then assumed I was sleeping with some man for a place to stay. I proudly responded that I had my own place even though I knew it didn't matter. It just felt good to say it. I told her that whatever was left throw it away because I won't be back. I said goodbye. She called me a few stupid bitches, said I wouldn't make it and when I didn't make it that I couldn't come back there either. I just looked at her and shook my head. I left. For good. Lord knows I really felt that way, but deep down I knew I couldn't stay away for two reasons: 1) my daddy and 2) my niece was there. She had become used to me being there to bathe her and put her to sleep. So, I had to wean her into me no longer being there.

Life was good! I had my own place, in school, worked periodically, due to public assistance, hung out with my friends...and still in church. My birthday came and I am now TWENTY. Since I started college, my friends and I would plan bus trips to Virginia, and this year was no different. We usually would do the package deal of either two amusement parks or a park and Virginia Beach. This trip was Busch Gardens and Kings Dominion. While in Virginia, I called my mother because I wanted to speak to my niece on my day, even though she was only two and I knew she was waiting to hear from me. I braced myself for whatever I had to listen to before I spoke to her. Heck, I wasn't even sure if she would let me speak to my niece once she knew it was me on the other end. My mother answered the phone, and to my surprise, she was cordial! I almost hung up and called again! I mean, she said happy birthday and everything! She even gave me a speech of how I left a child and would be returning back a woman. WOW! I was looking at the phone like it was a ghost. I looked around my hotel room to see if anyone else was in the room trying to play a joke on me, but I was in there all by myself. I'll take that over chocolate cake any day! Thank you, God for small miracles!

After speaking with my niece, I decided that when I returned back from Virginia, I would go to my mother's house. Whelp, a small miracle was exactly what it was. When I arrived at my mother's house, the door couldn't shut behind me fast enough before she started in with the cussing and negativity. What happened to the speech and the tears? It was only 24 hours ago. Really? I felt so sucker punched. Based on the speech she gave while I was in Virginia, I actually thought we could just be cordial, and maybe finally build some type of relationship, especially since I was no longer living there. But no. Not now. Not ever. I just simply went and got my niece and we went out for a few hours. We went to our favorite place, McDonalds. Not only was it our favorite place, but it was the only place opened that time of night. My niece wanted to be a big girl so I stood her up on the counter, put money in her hand, and let her "pay" for everything. We ate and sang and danced and had a good time until it was time to leave. It pained me to take my niece back to my mother and leave her there, but I wasn't completely stable to keep her with me. After that, visits to my mother's house were scarce. I am totally convinced that no matter what, my mother was never going to want me or love me and there was nothing I can do about it, but accept it.

It has been about a year since I moved into my own place and everything was pretty good. We had endless company, boyfriends would come over, and we cooked up a storm. We would do silly stuff like I would call Lei on the phone, ask her what she was doing or if she was hungry, and then we would meet in the kitchen. What's funny about that? Our rooms were literally across from each other. All I had to do was open the door and talk to her but no, we executed being footloose and fancy free to the utmost! We just didn't know how to not have fun! Then one day Lei came home from work and was so sad, nervous and panicky. She definitely had been crying. She had lost her job. Yep, company downsized and she was no longer needed. Because I was the one who was on public assistance, I always considered her the stable one. So now what? We discussed it and the conclusion was she was going back home to her parents, and I had to either find another roommate or another place to live. We went and met with the landlord and he and his wife agreed and decided that they didn't want someone else there so I definitely had to leave. They were very supportive and assisted in every way they could. I didn't realize it then but I remember depression engulfing me until I just dropped out of school. Unlike Lei, I could not go back to my mother's house. The thought of that sickened me every time I thought about it or someone suggested it. I remembered God promising me through his word that He would take care of me so I decided to trust His word even though I didn't fully understand what trusting in God really meant. All I know is that God made a way for me to leave my mother's house of torment, and I was sure He was aware of what was going on, and would see me through this trauma as well....I hoped. Apartment/room hunting was not easy when you are pressed for time, and have to meet a deadline. I was panicking and trying not to fully give in to this depression. So when I don't know what to do, I walk.

One day I went for a walk with no destination in mind. My

head was hanging down, tears flowing because it was close to the day I had to leave my first home, and I hadn't found anything or anywhere as of yet. All kinds of anxieties and thoughts of suicide were racing through my mind, along with all that my mother said before I left her house. When I finally looked up, I was crossing Bronx River Pkwy. As I was about to cross the street, someone was calling out my name as they were exiting off the parkway. It was a relative, a cousin on my daddy's side of the family who I had not seen in years! She pulled over and we talked for a few and just that quick, after I explained my situation, she offered me a place to stay at her house with her mom, my older cousin/auntie! God did it again! He kept on making a way for me! I think I was starting to get the hang of this trust thing! Thank you Lord, for making a way for me again!!!

This next move was also a part of a major transition in my life. Not only did I leave my mother's house, and had to leave my first apartment, but I also left my family church in the Bronx. Nothing bad had happened. I just felt there was more to God than I had been taught, so I set out to find it....and find it I did!!! After much convincing from a friend, I started attending a very prestigious church in Harlem. And just like that, after a few visits on Sunday mornings and Friday night Bible studies, I united with this ministry. God had my life back on track. I was learning and growing more in God. I came off public assistance, and went back to work. I was safe at my cousin/auntie house...so I thought. Being that it was "family" you would think there would be a lot of support and understanding; and it was at first. Then I started to notice that my space for rent would waver according to situations that had nothing to do with me. When I first moved in, let's say the rent we agreed on was $100 per week. But then some weeks it was $125, $135, etc. It was hardly ever $100 like we agreed. It wasn't long before I figured out that my cousin/auntie was charging me rent according to her extracurricular activity expenses per week. The more she indulged, the more my rent would be. On the weeks I didn't have what she asked for and I only had what we agreed on, there was always the threat of being put out. Here I am again living in fear. Not only that but I started to hear my mother's voice every time something went wrong. Here I was again with that constant reminder that nobody wanted me. The sting of failure was front and vivid like I had never even left my mother's house. Once again, I was only happy and free at church, and uncomfortable and hating where I lived. I didn't even realize that I was living a double life. I was victorious and fearless in church, but the complete opposite at home. I couldn't understand how a voice could have so much control over my emotions and my life. How did I get in this predicament again?

I need thee, O, I need thee,
Ev'ry hour I need thee,
Bless me now my savior,
I come, I come to thee.

Well the good thing was that I noticed the pattern of

selfishness and disrespect immediately. After a few verbal run-ins with my cousin/auntie we both agreed it was time for me to go. The last thing I was going to do was be totally disrespectful to someone who opened their doors to me, but at the same time I was not going to allow anyone to take advantage of me. And here I was again, walking and talking with God, and still holding Him at His word. And here He goes AGAIN keeping His promise to take care of me! Through the church realm, I befriended a young lady through a mutual friend who was in the midst of a horrible situation. I needed a place to stay and she just needed help. Period. And just like that I believe the Bible says suddenly. We both had exactly what we needed. God is forever sovereign! He knows just when to provide for His chosen. This set up was superb and perfect. Now if I can just get rid of that negative voice that tormented me daily....

As I became older, me and the brood, remember them, became close. We realized and agreed that we didn't choose this life for ourselves, and we were not each other's enemy. We were brothers and sisters. The funniest thing was whenever we spoke of Jeanine, we all addressed her as Jeanine. Not ma, not mommy, not mother. Just Jeanine. Then one day in September of 1995, one of them, possibly my sister, called me to say that Jeanine was in the hospital, and she was asking to see us. She had been diagnosed with Tuberculosis and wasn't doing too well. With all that she was dealing with I thought the report would have been worse. At least that explained why she coughed like a lumber jack with a bad cold. We all met up to discuss who was going to see her. That conversation was crazy! Nobody wanted to go, but knew we had to go. I definitely had to go because at the time I think I was the only one in church, therefore labeled as the Christian in the family. Talk about being stuck between a rock and hard place! And what was even crazier was that she was in the hospital, literally three blocks from my church. REALLY Jesus? You would do this to me??? I was so distraught with my decision of whether or not to go see a complete stranger, that one Sunday I was compelled to speak to one of my choir members about the situation. Ironically, she had to deal with the same issue concerning her dad. After speaking with her, I made my decision.

When I arrived home, I called my siblings, and we all agreed to meet at the hospital after work. We all kept our word and arrived like we said, but we weren't allowed to see her. We were too late. Jeanine had transcended earlier that day. We stood there with the well at least we did come look on our faces. We didn't have a reason to reminisce or take a walk down memory lane simply because she didn't raise us. There was no need for us to even shed a tear. We were so detached that we couldn't even fake it. I cried and mourned the death of Whitney Houston more than I did Jeanine. Me and my siblings promised to stay in touch and departed. Even though I didn't attend the service, I believe my siblings did. The only reason I went by her funeral in the first place was to make sure my daddy and my brother made it. You see, by this time, he was placed in a nursing home by his sisters due to him being diagnosed with Alzheimer's disease. And my brother, well he was renting a room in a beautiful gated community. I never went inside, I didn't view the body, and I didn't sign the book. I waited for my daddy outside and once I saw that he was okay, I left. At this point, I would have felt more comfortable had I chosen a complete stranger from a newspaper listing than staying there for Jeanine.

Should auld acquaintance be forgot,
And never brought to mind,
Should auld acquaintance be forgot
And auld lang syne.

Being that there was no bond, no connection, no attachment, moving on from this moment in my life would be easy. I wish I could tell you that it was. The truth is, it was one of the hardest things I ever had to deal with. It wasn't until she was dead and buried that I had questions. Now I wanted to talk. Why didn't you want me? Why were you a secret? Why all of my siblings had an opportunity to be with you and call you mommy? How were you able to be around me for six years before I accidentally found out the truth? Had that moment never happened, would I have ever been told the truth? Who is my biological father? These questions opened yet another portal or level of feeling unwanted. Maybe I should have made more of an effort to try and listen to her side of the story. Maybe I should have tried a little harder to at least be cordial. Maybe I should have made more of an effort to be her friend.   Maybe things would have turned out a little better than they did. Maybe. Bad enough I had to deal with tuning out my mother's voice of negativity, now I had to fight against my own thoughts of not being worthy of love or even good enough to be around. How do you stand strong against the negativity when the facts are stronger? I found myself crying more and praising God even harder, whether I believed it or not. It's been said to fake it until you make it so that's just what I was going to do. I was going to live my life as if I was happy until my life actually becomes that life of happiness I so desire.

My friend that I lived with also had children, 2 toddlers to be exact.   Her children were now my children.   She trusted me completely. Our relationship was amazing. It was as if we knew each other all our lives. As usual, I was watching them while she was at work. No one really knew what I was dealing with or how strong these feelings were that kept me emotionally captive. This particular day, I couldn't even care for the children. As soon as she left, I fed them and a few minutes later I made them lay down for a nap. When I was convinced that they were good and sound asleep, I went to the bathroom and proceeded to do the most unchristian act you could imagine. I opened the medicine cabinet, took a razor, went in the bedroom, closed the door and began to cut my right wrist.   So here I was crying, cutting, praying and bleeding. At that time, I felt it was the only solution. I was tired of faking it as if everything was alright. IT WASN'T! I was tired of pretending that I was alright. And why wouldn't I be?

Because I had free room and board and meals; and because temping assignments were few and far in between. I went back on public assistance and literally took care of her children and home, while my friend regrouped and got her life back on track. So, I should be leaping for joy. Was this not the promise of God that He would provide for me? He kept His word, so why am I cutting my wrist? I was cutting my wrist because I wasn't at a level of trusting God where He would heal me emotionally.

Remember I said the children were good and sound asleep??? How about while I am cutting myself, the youngest child woke up and came in the room with a Barney tape asking to watch it!!! WHAT KID???? ARE YOU SERIOUS??? Why are you here?! You are supposed to be asleep!!! BARNEY?!?! I was so engulfed with my thoughts that it was too late to undo what was already in progress. The child saw me crying and the blood, said I had a "boo-boo" and tried to find me a band-aid. When the child left the room I asked God why He interrupted the process. I didn't understand or embrace it then, but I understand and embrace it now. I couldn't commit suicide because purpose wouldn't let me die. When God has a mandate on your life, there is absolutely nothing you can do about it. The child came back with a wash cloth, and did her best to take care of me. I told her I felt much better and we went to watch Barney. That incident caused me to become closer to God and challenged me to believe that God had need of me. Since the incident, my love and fire for God was on ten plus! The internal mental battles still existed, but the more I learned of God a little easier it became.

In July of 1997, I received some heartbreaking news. My favorite uncle, my twin Vonné's daddy, had died. He was my uncle, boyfriend, bodyguard, banker and best friend all wrapped up into one. But most importantly, he was my refuge when my mother was beyond out of control. My uncle and my mother argued often about me. My mother hated being told she was wrong. Many nights I had to call for him to come get and save me before I was able to move out on my own. Or either he would find me just sitting in front of his door, sleep like a crackhead because I didn't want to be at home with my mother. Many of his dates ended sooner than planned because of me. Thanks Unc for putting me first. Then in October of 1997 I received more bad news, my auntie, my uncle's sister, had died just a few days before my uncle's birthday. Good grief, what was this, a conspiracy? I was still grieving my uncle and now this. She was another house of refuge that helped keep my sanity when my mother felt the need to audition for the G building. She was the cool one in the family. Everybody was always at her house. My auntie was just a party all by herself. Most of the time, people thought I was her child. These are actually Doris' children, not Jeanine's siblings. I was beginning to feel lonely and defenseless against my mother, even though I was grown and no longer in her house. It was just good to know that I had someone in my corner besides my daddy who knew my mother was not playing with a full deck. May they continue to rest in peace. Love you.

HAPPY NEW YEAR! WHEW! It's 1998 and after last year, I am looking forward to a little happiness, Amen?! As I was adjusting to back-to-back deaths, I was also concluding my 90 days probation on my new job! I was the administrative assistant at a very prestige financial firm in Manhattan. I was so proud of myself. This year was off to a great start, until I answered the phone. It was one of my siblings, my sister actually, telling me something I couldn't quite comprehend. She called to tell me that my mother had died. HUH? WHAT? REPEAT THAT PLEASE??? There were too many emotions going on at one time that I couldn't keep up. I knew my sister wouldn't lie about something like that, but I still called a few people to confirm. They confirmed her death, but didn't think enough of me to let me know she was in the hospital two weeks before her death. Excuse me??? Who left you HNIC of my life when you can't take care of you and yours???!!!! Regardless of what may have happened between her and I, that was STILL MY MOTHER and you had no right to take that from me. I remember being dazed and crying with disbelief when I went to tell my boss. After speaking with her, she released me for the rest of the day, but I was scared to leave my boss. She was crying harder than I was. Once she pulled herself together, I went straight to Bronx Lebanon Hospital with my childhood bestie. They told me the doctor left for the day, but they did call and let me speak with him. He asked me to come back in the morning. Lord, I haven't been on the block in almost ten years since my daddy was placed in a hospice. I called my godmother and stayed with her. I didn't sleep well at all. I was overly consumed with disbelief, hatred, joy, relief, peace, confusion, rest, betrayal, anger and unanswered questions again. But right now, I had to check all of that at the door because I had business to take care of in the morning. Promptly at 9am my god sister and I were at the hospital to meet with my mother's doctor. Now I told y'all my mother had bronchial asthma, right? So why was this man telling me that my mother died from cancer??? He showed me her files and there it was in black and white: my mother had developed lung cancer. That's why she stopped smoking. I guess to preserve her life, too little, too late. I asked to see her. He looked at me strangely as if I didn't know what a morgue was. He told me that this was not normal procedure, and once I go view, no other family members can see her. I told him I was the family. With a blank stare, he asked us to follow him.

We go down in the basement and they bring her body out. I was looking at my mother through a partition lying on a cold metal rolling table, covered with a white sheet. I couldn't touch her or go in. I just could view her through the glass. My god sister didn't know what to expect, and quite honestly neither did I. All I could do was just stand there and stare at her. I couldn't believe that this was my mother lying on that cold metal table, not talking or cussing me out. "Nah, she just sleep or in a light coma. She's gonna wake up" is what I was telling myself while staring at her. Wait! Did her eye just twitch?! Okay, think Cherise, think. Everyone at Bronx Lebanon Hospital knows who the Stevenson's are, literally. So if your mother was just asleep, why is she in the morgue when we all know asthmatic patients are on the seventh floor? Is this really how this relationship was going to end? I don't remember how long I was standing there, but had to be for some time because the doctor came after a while to ask if I was alright. I said yeah, I'm just waiting for her to send me to the store for her beer. She always sent me to the store. I believe my god sister cussed and that's when the doctor told her to come get me. As we were about to leave, the doctor wanted to give me my mother's belongings: her housecoat, reading glasses and a tri-colored diamond encrusted ring that I gave her for Mother's Day some years ago. I didn't know at the time of purchase it was actually a wedding band. Because of the lifestyles of my relatives, I remember her saying that she would never take that ring off, and it would be over her dead body before they took it and sold it for a quick high. It was at the sight of that ring that I passed out. It had hit me that my mother was dead. When they helped me up off of the floor, they had no idea the state of mind I was in. If the doctor could have discerned it, he would have admitted me immediately. But I couldn't show my true emotions because I had business to attend to and family to deal with. Being that I was not the beneficiary for anything, my business was handled within a day and that was to call housing and other bill collectors and close everything down. Because of my cousin's activities, my mother's service was in a funeral home in Harlem, and she was placed in a light blue cardboard box, not even a casket. She was dressed in some yellow suit that was too big for her, and wasn't from her closet. After that her body just laid in the morgue because they were waiting for the balance of payment from my cousin. They couldn't wait any longer so my mother was put to rest two weeks later in Potter's Field. Yes, Potter's Field is a real place for those who can't afford proper burial. Now that all has been taken care of I could get back to life as normal, right???

Internally, I was still decomposing. I say still because it initially started when I first heard the news of my mother's death. Once I was home and finally able to sit still, I thought I would be able to be on one accord mind, body and soul with myself. Logically I should have been preparing to return back to work. I had no real reason to continue to mourn. After all, she didn't want me either. We didn't have a bond, closeness, a connection. She just raised me. Reality is that her death took me into the abyss of depression for months. Not only did I end up losing my job, but I lost my sense of self and of life. I just sat in the house and just waited to die. I had asked my boss to please let me return to work because I needed something to do. She insisted that I take more time off and return when I was absolutely ready. That day of me being absolutely ready never came. I just simply never called again and never went back. I remember not eating, barely bathing and many sleepless nights of just sitting on the couch. All the church I attended, all the God I had learned about didn't stop this indescribable moment that I was experiencing. I heard it said that earth has no sorrow that heaven cannot heal. Does that mean that this indescribable, unbearable, emotional struggle wasn't

45

going to end until I reached heaven? Does that mean until that time, I have to suffer here on earth? What does it mean to not let your heart be troubled when it's been troubled since the age of 14? WHAT DO THESE SCRIPTURES MEAN??? AND HOW ARE THEY GOING TO HELP ME NOW???!!! How could verbal and emotional abuse be so loud and controlling from the grave? Now my questions were asking questions and I would respond with negativity. Apparently, my mother was right.

DECADE FOUR – 2000'S: "INTENTIONAL SURVIVAL"

Ephesians 3:20 "Now unto Him that is able to do exceeding abundantly above all that we ask or think according to the power that worketh in us..."

All things are working for my good
He's intentional, never failing
I don't have to worry cause
It's working for me – Travis Greene

I opened this segment of story with strong positivity because I believe everything that has happened to me was intentional through the power of God – even situations that I may have caused on my own.

After my mother died, things became worse. I no longer cared about life. Once I lost my job, there was a lot of tension and eventually I was asked to leave. There really was no need for me anymore. My friend had gotten her life together: graduated college and landed an awesome job; children were school aged, plus with after school programs I was left with nothing to do or anyone to care for. However, I managed to stay in church and the new ministry that I was now a part of was predicated on prayer and praise. Even though I was a dressed-up mess, attending this church probably saved my life. Prayer and praise was keeping me committed and connected to God. Prayer and praise helped me become refocused and renewed. I started believing what God said about me. Started believing I was more than a conqueror. I can do all things through Christ who strengthen me. I am fearfully and wonderfully made. I was on my way to recovery and wholeness. I was even smiling again! I was enjoying and trusting Jesus again! In the midst of all this joy, I became reacquainted with a friend. Little did I know they were my guardian angel (GA).

Shortly after I connected with GA, I lost my job and was put out of my place again. The irony in that was my boss was also my landlord and I was renting a room out of her apartment in the projects. She didn't fire me for lack of job performance or disciplinary actions at work. It was for personal reasons. She fired me because she was three months pregnant, but her boyfriend didn't want the baby so he kicked her in her stomach and she fell down the stairs. What did that have to do with me? I beat his behind on her behalf and she chose her man over me, her friend, so I thought. Beat him good, too. And because failure was the gateway of my mother's negativity, immediately my mother's voice of negativity was all I heard and all I wanted to do was die. Once I told GA, they assured me that everything was going to be alright. They reminded me of all I had survived and God was not going to let it end like this. GA was right. Within a few weeks, thanks to GA, I had a new job and a new place. And still God was keeping His promise to me! My gratefulness unto God was on ten every day! When I gave up on Him, He not only did not give up on me, but He yet looked beyond my faults, saw my needs and provided for me! I am now safe and established with a new home and job. I also went back to school to complete my B.A. and I was in Bible school through my church. I was excelling at everything. God is good.

It is now Monday, December 3, 2001. As I was finishing up my class in Bible school, a member of the church found me and I could tell something wasn't right. As they approached me I could tell they didn't have a choice in the matter of being the messenger, especially because of our bond outside of church was not a pleasant one. "Your aunt said to call her" was the message. I stared at them for a minute because their eyes were saying what their mouth couldn't. Even though there was much distance between us, I could tell they didn't want to deliver this particular message, even if it would have given them the opportunity to gloat a little. I said okay and thanked them for the message. I stood still for a moment even as there were many people passing by me, I felt completely alone. I snapped out of the trance immediately before the "are you alright" questions started for fear that I would lose my composure. As my friend drove me home, they noticed the change in facial expression and body language. "What's wrong?" Oh, nothing. I was just told that my daddy died. Because they didn't know what to say or do, we rode in silence all the way to my house. I couldn't tell them how I felt or what I needed because I didn't know. That was the day the earth stood still. Everyone that knew about my relationship with my daddy knew he was the dot on the letter "I" and the cross on the letter "T". God in all His wisdom knew that as well, which is why he brought comfort to my soul about my daddy's death six months before it happened. It was a Tuesday night in May and we were in prayer. While praying, God allowed me to actually see my daddy's funeral. I cried straight through the night into the next day. Immediately after that, I went to see him, not realizing that it was also his 80th birthday. So even though the news that it had finally come to pass was detrimental, I was already at peace with it. However, my mind and my heart struggled with it a little. My heart was concerned about me having that support, protection and counsel that only a daddy can give especially since I was not married. For the first time, I felt completely alone. Lord knows I miss my daddy every day since his transition. May he continue to rest in peace. I love you, daddy.

As it is soon approaching time for me to take my final exams from both schools, I informed those in authority that I would not be in Tuesday night Bible study and prayer service. I would be home preparing for my finals. It may have been around 11 or 11:30pm at night when my phone started ringing non-stop. When I answered it was a friend of mine asking me why I didn't tell her that I was excommunicated from the church?! HUH???? MISS??? WHAT ARE YOU TALKING ABOUT?! I was still a member of the church! I was just home studying for my finals! Apparently, I did something that pastor wasn't pleased with, and he kicked me out the church while I was home. What did I do? Until this day, I honestly have no idea; I have some speculations, but nothing concrete. I was very disappointed behind that because I was one of them that served him closely. He knew me by my full name. I had never missed a service, rehearsal, meeting, conference, nothing. If whatever I did bothered him so much, the least he could have done was met with me face to face as opposed to acting out in his own feelings while his goons edged him on. With the exception of funerals of some very close friends of mine from that ministry, I haven't been back for anything. Maybe one day I will, but until then life goes on. I am a strong believer that if you are in the right, then there is no need for you to fight, prove yourself or defend yourself. Isaiah 59:19 says "...when the enemy shall come in like a flood, the spirit of the Lord shall lift up a standard against him." That's God's job. God will always vindicate what's right. And yes, I have been vindicated over and over again. There is no hatred in my heart and I forgive him. Hopefully one day I will be able to tell him that face to face. I forced myself to complete my finals before I gave myself over to grief. And yes, I passed my classes both academically and in bible school. I made the dean's list with a GPA of 3.74 academically and I received all A's from bible school.

Grief comes in many forms, shapes and fashion. Even though I looked and felt okay, I really wasn't. I remember wanting to be in a relationship really bad to fill the void of my daddy. Every time a relationship failed, it would be the voice of my mother telling me it didn't work because I wasn't good enough and no man would ever want me. Then the cycle flipped! I no longer wanted the closeness and intimacy of a relationship. I just wanted what I wanted, and then you had to go. I felt the pain would be less if I got rid of the guy before he tried to get rid of me. I literally became the guy. Then I didn't want to be with anyone. This was the cycle of my life for the next couple of years. I was also living from pillow to post, couch to floor. I had a piece of a job here and a piece there or nothing at all. I was about one friend away from being homeless. I even moved out of New York for a season only to return back to the vicious cycle all over again. It was upon returning back to NY that I learned you can't conquer anything if you first don't confront it. And yes, GA was still there, but there was only so much they could do. When you are fighting against yourself internally, help from others will not prevail. This is where tough love is applied and we pray for the right outcome. No one, not even me, knew what my mood would be from day to day. I would be happy today, mad tomorrow. I would be a conqueror today, defeated tomorrow. I would love you today, hate you tomorrow. When I was up, I was way up, but when I was down, it was over. Either I was going to hurt you or myself, but somebody was gonna get it. I was just a big bag of emotions fighting internal demons that I really didn't understand at that time. As far as I was concerned, I was just having a bad day, but every day, though??? This destructive mental behavior went on for years. And all the while I was still in church. This is why we need to be careful how we treat people. You have no idea what they are going through. I remember wanting to commit suicide often, but would go to church first as a "last" resort. I remember lying in my bed for days totally disconnected from the world waiting to die because I couldn't get it together. I didn't know how to stop the verbal and emotional abuse in my mind. Therefore, I concluded, as usual, my mother was right about me.

After many, many years of tossing and turning, sleepless nights and angry days, I decided that I needed to speak to someone who could really help me. Not that my friends or even my GA didn't try and help, but I needed an answer that would break me. I went back to my spiritual uncle and auntie's church in the Bronx. Why them? Because it was them so many years ago that answered my how questions: How do I live right? How do I really trust God beyond just saying that I do? How is God going to forgive that? How do I know God's voice? How do I know my purpose? If they could help me get an understanding of all of that, surely they could help me get over this internal battle. So here I was back in the Bronx with my family, still stand-offish. I just wanted God, some answers and then go home, A-men? This was my last resort. If they couldn't help me then I just couldn't be helped. Remember a few pages back I said I was in church and I learned God? Well, it was here that I learned how to apply God. It was here where I learned to confront and conquer. Being back here, I was able to see the application of God through the transparency of my aunt and uncle. It was here that I was able to become vulnerable enough to be broken and deal with my past issues. Please understand this was not easy and probably the most difficult thing anyone would have to do. Salvation is free, but deliverance takes work! This is why I say it is difficult, but not impossible! Not only do you have to be willing to put in the work but more importantly, you have to want to be delivered. You have to be consistent. You have to understand that deliverance is not going to happen in twenty minutes because you finally admitted unto God that you need to be delivered. I literally had to force myself to focus on what God said about me and tune out all the past negative statements that were said by my mother and now anyone else that would say bad things about me or to me. I had to stand up in my own truth and believe that I am somebody, and I will have all God intended for me to have according to His will over my life. It's like a verbal tug-o-war going on in my mind. The only thing that kept me going was that I finally believed that this is what God wanted for me as well. I believed that the more I wanted to be delivered from negativity the more God would help me because the bible says that God will give you the desires of your heart. (Psalm 37:4)

While in my spiritual process, God was taking care of some natural, everyday things in my life, like employment. It wasn't until this incident that I understood divine connection. One day while in church a woman walked over to me and asked if I was working. I said no and she told me about some test. She would ask me every week literally, until I finally took the stupid test! Let's just say thank you to her for making me take that stupid test. Because of her persistence, and me taking that stupid test in 2008, I am employed today! And that was just the beginning of the walls of self-defeat beginning to crumble in my life! Things were finally coming together for me. Shortly after that, I remember a Sunday afternoon service where my auntie came over to me and called me forth into ministry as an Evangelist in 2009. After many transitions, I was finally licensed in 2014. After having many addresses and sometimes not having one at all, God finally settled me with my own beautiful place in 2011. Even my apartment has its own testimony: after many letters of rejection, I went to see this particular place. I didn't have a choice in the matter because basically this apartment was assigned to me. So if I didn't like it, I was placed back on the bottom of the waiting list. I loved it of course, went to the management office to sign my lease and walked out with my keys to my new place WITHOUT GIVING THEM ANY MONEY!!! Nobody but God can do something like that! I also remember sitting in bible study on a Wednesday night in the fall of 2009. While my uncle was teaching, God dropped in my spirit to write a book, not just any book, this book. The more I was becoming free from this internal battle, the more the enemy would try to rise up against me to discourage me. And let me be honest, sometimes he would win, but the difference now is, I activate my God given power that is within me to overcome the tactics of the enemy. I learned that my words have POWER and I have to use my words wisely. I learned that you have to speak what you want in your life over your life.

If you keep calling someone stupid, eventually they are not going to strive or set goals for themselves because they already believe that they are stupid so why try. But if you want to be free from emotional bondage and break generational curses over your life, then speak life free of all that has kept you from reaching your greatest potential. The bible says, "death and life are in the power of the tongue and they that love it shall eat the fruit thereof," Proverbs 18:21. The next time someone says you can't or you won't, tell them to just watch. "Greater is He that is within you, than he that is in the world," I John 4:4. Activate your God-given power within you and watch God move on your behalf. And the only way to activate your God-given power is to read and stay in the word of God. Always seal your power with prayer and praise.

I realize now that all of what I have gone through and survived was for YOU. Someone needs to know that they are not crazy and yes, they can overcome their internal struggles. God allowed me this experience because sometimes in order to be an affective witness you have to be your own crash dummy to see if the product really works. I want you to know that God is a never-failing God. He knows what you need before you do. Just like Lamentations 3:23 says "great is thy faithfulness, O, Lord unto me." I stand as a true witness that no weapon formed against me shall prosper; and every tongue that shall rise against me in judgement, You (God) shall condemn," Isaiah 54:17. I was able to survive because God was standing up in me. Now I am able to live because I stand up in Him. I wrote this to testify that God is real and He works. I am healed from bitterness and hatred, and I now love and believe in myself. I don't have a fairytale ending, but I do have a God-ever-after ending for Philippians 1:6 states "Being confident of this very thing, that He who has begun a good work in you will complete it until the day of Jesus Christ!"

My mother was wrong.

ABOUT THE AUTHOR

Cherise Stevenson is a native New Yorker who was born and raised in the Bronx, and now resides in Brooklyn. Cherise has attended prestigious schools such as Lehman College and Long Island University; soon to complete her BA in Business Administration. Cherise sung with world renowned choirs such as Bishop Hezekiah Walker and the Love Fellowship Choir, Bishop Eric McDaniel and The Lord's Church Choir, Pastor Maharold Peoples and Worship and Praise, and The Pilgrim Cathedral of Harlem Church Choir. In August 2014, Cherise was licensed as an Evangelist by Bishop James A. Jones Sr. of Divine Destiny Christian Center. In her spare time, Cherise enjoys event planning, but her ultimate passion is children and the things of God. Her favorite confession is, "I love the Lord and I won't take it back."

Made in the USA
Middletown, DE
23 July 2020